Living and Teaching

On

Saint Thomas

In The

United States Virgin Islands

Published by DryHeatPublishing, LLC 2017

© Larry Brasen 2017   ISBN: 978-0-578-19308-3

Our U.S.V.I

When we were what appeared to be a safe distance from the Eastern shore of St. Thomas, we killed the engine on the little sloop and went about hoisting the jib and the mainsail. I didn't take into account the ever present Easterly wind blowing us toward the shore. Since we hadn't practiced it at anchor, there were a couple of hitches in our get-alongs for which we were not fully prepared. Half way up the mast our jib got fouled in the jib track. As we were all trying to work on the jib, we didn't notice that the Easterly was pushing us gradually toward the shore where the waves were crashing on boulders. We got the jib up and started hoisting the mainsail when I became aware of the sound of a tremendous crashing of waves on the rocks. I glanced over at the shore and was shocked to see the white foam being thrown into the air. My God!!! I could even distinguish the plant life growing on the huge volcanic boulders. I started pulling the starter rope on the outboard motor and of course the miserable thing wouldn't catch. We were less than a block away from the shore. Just as we were about to die in the boating accident of the year…

How in the world did two school teachers and their ten year old son from Montana get into this extremely dangerous situation? Could this near death experience have been foreseen and avoided?

Prologue

Grasshopper Summer

Ants work all the summer,

Grasshoppers only play.

When life hands you a bummer,

Go the grasshopper way.

    Nineteen seventy-one! What an interesting year. I had effectively been fired from my job as music instructor at Eureka High School, in Eureka, Montana. Even though after some reconsideration the school board decided to rehire me I wasn't about to continue teaching where I was apparently not wanted by several of the board members. So Betty, Larry Jr. and I were at loose ends.

    We decided to have a party for the summer. Grasshoppers that we were, we went to Helena, the Capital of Montana, to the Montana Retirement System to pull out all the retirement savings I had and just relax and try to reassemble our lives somehow. We all walked into the government office with a feeling of ownership. This was, after all, OUR office. WE paid for it. It was MY money. If we felt like doing this it was obviously OUR business.

    "How may I help you today"? Asked the slightly overweight clerk behind the counter.

"I'm here to pull my money out of the retirement system", I replied.

"Oh, really? May I see the form signed by your school Clerk of the Board"? She asked.

"What is this now? I don't have any form of any kind signed by anybody. I just want my money. I never needed to have a form before."

With her head shaking from side to side just a little, eyebrows arched, and nose pointing to the heavens she said, "It has been that way for two years now. I'm surprised you didn't know".

This was really putting a monkey wrench in my plans for a "Grasshopper Summer." We had already started making plans, we had driven all the way to Helena, we had walked into an office I thought we owned, and now THIS! I had just had it! "That's just what's wrong with this deal. You say you want to attract teachers to the profession. (Louder) No wonder people don't go into teaching. It's all this MICKEY MOUSE CRAP we have to put up with!" I was yelling.

I heard a small snicker. I looked around. At nine Larry Jr. knew who Mickey Mouse was. He apparently also knew what Crap was. I guess he had never had the mental picture that came from putting them together. I started laughing and Betty started laughing. The clerk was stifling a giggle. Tears actually came to my eyes as I started to visualize Mickey Mouse Crap.

When the hilarity calmed down the clerk phoned the necessary party in Eureka to insure I was no longer employed there and processed the retirement money. So we started our "Grasshopper Summer".

Betty's Sister, Alida's House

The summer wore on as we visited all the old haunts, family, people around Montana that we knew and liked. We were just coming up with the idea that it would be good to find a job for the following year. Our money was already beginning to run low. Eastern Montana College of Education was located in Billings, Montana. We both graduated from that institution and all our professional paperwork was located there as well as their Educational Placement Office.

Betty's sister Alida was living in Billings with her two little children, Jenny and Jeff. Her husband, Al, was serving in the Air Force in Viet Nam. We called and she invited us to stay with her while we looked for jobs. We spent a couple days catching up and then I was ready to test the employment waters.

In the dressiest summer attire I could muster up, I appeared at the College Placement Office. As I introduced myself to the lady in charge, I noticed the name Mrs. Bernardi on her identification pin. I had worked the previous summer in the Eastern Montana College Summer Theatre Workshop. An assistant professor that I had worked closely with and had admired greatly had been named Jim Bernardi. Of course I asked and was informed that she was Jim's wife. She said she remembered me in the role of "Judd Fry" in <u>Oklahoma!</u> I couldn't believe my good fortune. This might just work out after all.

She showed me the job opening desk and posting board. Each Montana school that had a vacancy for a music teacher was listed. There were several Class C schools that fit the description. My problem was I had just been employed in a Class B school and I didn't want to step backwards into a C school. Of course if it meant the difference between being employed in a school or having to query the ubiquitous, "Would you like fries with that sir"? I would be happy to take the Class C School. I also felt as though I had already "been there, done that" and this would just be a repeat of the previous years with new faces.

"Are you seeing anything at all interesting?" asked Sandy.

Shaking my head up and down and sideways at the same time I mumbled, "Yeah…No…uhh…Sandy, I think I am looking for something a little more…out of the ordinary. You know? Something…well sort of different. I don't really know what I'm talking about, do I?"

"You know, there was a notice in my church bulletin I read yesterday. They are looking for teachers in the Virgin Islands. What do you think of that"?

"Wow", I said a little louder than necessary. "What, Where, Uh, Virgin Islands? Hey, what do I need to do?"

"I'll tell you what. That bulletin is at home. I'll bring it in tomorrow if you want and you'll be able to look it over."

I couldn't hide a little grin. "I'll be back tomorrow morning. What time do you open?"

I couldn't wait to tell Betty.

At home now, "Hon, they have openings in the Virgin Islands!"

"The Virgin Islands? Where are they? Betty asked.

"I have no idea, but it does sound interesting, doesn't it?"

At this point Alida, who had heard the exchange said, "The Virgin Islands were featured in one of my last National Geographics. They are down in the basement. Let's go down and dig through them until we find the issue."

The article located the island group in the Caribbean not far from Puerto Rico. The pictures were of course gorgeous. "Wow! I can't believe we could be going to the Virgin Islands," I said.

"Do they need Music Teachers and Reading Specialists"? asked Betty.

"I don't have any idea. We'll just have to wait until tomorrow to find out more."

Early the next day Sandy handed me a copy of the bulletin. It said a new Junior/Senior High School had been built and staffing was needed. Thanking Sandy, I returned home with the sketchy information. At least I had the phone number of the Department of Education in Charlotte Amalie, St. Thomas, U.S.V.I.

The Phone Call

    Allowing for three hours difference in time zones, I placed my call at 7:00 AM. The phone rang a couple of times and then was picked up by a lady whose voice was liquid butter. "Gu-**maw**nin. **De**paw**ment** of Edjuca**tion**, may I help **you**?"
    "Yes, my name is Larry Brasen and I'm calling about a job listing I saw in our church bulletin Sunday. It said you are hiring teachers. My wife and I are both interested in coming there and applying for jobs."
    The cholesterol laden voice replied, "Firs of all, do **nah** come **here wit**out signed con**tracs**. Dat would be a big **mis**take. Se**con**, you mus fill out de application paypahs and sen dem in wit you paypahs here for us to check. Den we can sen you con**tracs** for you to sign **be**fore you come here in per**son**."
    I was barely breathing. "We can send the paperwork to you today. How long before we will know if we get jobs?
    "No hur**ry**, Mis**ta** Braaz. Ver soon. Where you do live?"
    "We live in Montana. In the United States."
    "Oh, My," She dripped. "My, my, my, my, my. So far away. So you tink you will like St. Toe**mas**? In de middle ob de sea?"
    I answered, "I **know** I'll love it. **We** will love it. I want to come there right now."
    "Oh, oh, oh. No rush. No hur**ry**. You jus sen de pay**pah** an we call **you**."
    "Okay. Here is my name and address. Can you send the application papers out today? We'll get them all filled out and sent back to you right away. I'll get my placement office to send you the papers today. If I don't hear from you in a week, would it be alright for me to give you a call and check in for an update?"
    "Of causs we bu**sy**, school star soon, but you can call any time you wan," she poured oleo on the earpiece.
    "Well, thanks a lot. See you soon. Bye. Oh, Oh, wait, wait a minute. Are you still there? When does school start there. When would we have to be there?

"We star in de terd **week** of Au**gus**", She replied.

"Wow, here we are in the third week of July. Can we get this whole thing taken care of in time?"

"You muss **re**lax. Tings happen in dae time here in de is**lans**. Tings can work out."

I heard these words come out of my mouth, "Relax, huh? (pause) Sounds good to me. (breath) Relax…(smile) Well, again, Thanks and goodbye."

"**Gou**-by, Mis**ta** Braaz."

The Wait

We returned to Eureka where our mobile home was parked. Our intention was to get everything prepared for the trip to the islands and prepare our home for rental. There were new teachers coming into Eureka that fall and we felt if we could rent for the monthly amount of our payments we would have no net loss on the house.

We were ready. Bags packed, ready to go. We were living in a Bob Dylan song. All our excess stuff was either stored or to be rented out. Two young lady teachers came and asked about renting the trailer. We showed them our home and discussed the agreement. They took it. Great! Now we pretty much had to get the jobs in the Virgin Islands. We wouldn't have a place to live. (Who was it that burned all the ships of his invading force and then commenced to plunder? There wouldn't be much plundering here but the ships had definitely been burned.)

Into the fourth week of July we had not heard anything from the V.I. I was getting a little concerned. "Betty, what do you think? Should I give them a call in the islands?"

I noticed her voice was a little higher and faster than usual. "I think it would be a great idea. Something could have been held up in the mail."

I phoned. They didn't have a record of sending anything to us. Good Grief! However, they were planning on sending it out that very day. Oh, my God. Time was running short. Didn't these people have any kind of a sense of time? We were to learn that they had a sense of time called "Virgin Island Time."

Check with Eastern Airlines. They served the V.I.

Check with the bank in Harlowton, Montana where we had an account to establish a line of credit for when we got to the islands.

We had a bit of a war council. "Look," I worried, "if that packet doesn't get here by the end of July. Let's say next Friday the 30th of July. If it doesn't get here by then, we'll just have to return to Billings and see what we can find. At this point beggars can't be choosers."

Betty agreed, "I'm with you. I know it will all work out in the long run."

The packet arrived on the 29th of July. We filled everything out and got it back in the mail the next day. We had a set of our placement papers from the college with us and included them with the pack. On Friday, the 30th of July 1971 we Air Mailed the packet and then sat back to wait. When you put all your eggs in one basket what happens if an elephant steps on it? Don't even go there.

In less than a week we received a phone call stating that Betty had a contract in the mail as a Reading Specialist. I hadn't been placed yet. I said we could live on one salary and I would write the "Great American Novel". Soon we would be on our way to the new life in the islands. Betty, Larry Jr. and I would each bring one large suitcase. In addition we brought two sets of golf clubs, my guitar and my Smith-Corona portable typewriter. Life was good!

Arrival

After changing planes in Minneapolis and Atlanta (for inexperienced travelers downright scary) and an overnight in Miami, we were finally on the last leg of this life changing flight. We had been flying over nothing but water for what seemed like hours. Well, it was hours. Now the stewardess was saying, "Buckle you seat belts… You are about to land at the Harry S. Truman Airport, Charlotte Amalie, Saint Thomas, United States Virgin Islands."

I looked out the window. There was no island. There was no land of any kind. There was nothing but water and the plane was only two feet off the waves. Okay! We're dead. All this distance to end like this. Hold on to Betty and Larry Jr. No way am I going to bend my head down like they said to do in an emergency. I may be a goner but I won't embarrass myself. I closed my eyes and waited for the fatal impact. The engines had cut way back. The wheels hit the tarmac and I opened my eyes. Just then the air brakes cut in and I about jumped out of my seat, buckle and all.

"Welcome to Saint Thomas," It was the stewardess. We were saved.

We taxied to a deplaning zone and came to a stop. Everyone was standing up, getting their belongings together to get off the plane. As we stood and prepared to see our new home for the first time, there was no way we could have been prepared for the first impression we were about to get. There was no concourse or jetway here. The stairway was deployed and the passengers were to walk to the interior of the airport. Our turn came to stand at the top of the stairway. The air was a dampened sponge that hit us in the face. It wasn't overly hot, just darned wet.

I glanced up at the airport tower. Two guys in tee shirts were lounging there leaning out of the windows. Oh, my God. Was this their version of Air Traffic Controllers? This was a powerful impression. Nothing happened in our time in the islands to change it. In fact that impression lasts to this very day.

The terminal was not far away, but by the time we reached it we were all soaked in sweat. After picking up our baggage (it all arrived safely) we made our way out of the terminal onto the main street. Taxi cabs were lined up for a block. The first cab driver said, "Gu Mawnin. Where you are goin today?"

Man, oh Man!!! "Pardon me?" I asked.

"Where you are go-**in**?"

"Oh," I said. I knew I was frowning slightly and thought it would be better if I tried to smile. Very slowly and a little louder with a lot of hesitation between the words, "We---Need---a---ho---tel!"

"Oh, you wan de Gran **Ho**tel. De ver Bes on de is**lan**. I take **you**. What you do **do** wit des tings here?" he asked as our belongings disappeared into the taxi's trunk.

"What, the golf clubs? You know what golf clubs are don't you? To play golf with?"

He replied, "Saint Croix," and shook his head.

I said, "Huh?"

He got behind the wheel and with a lot of gesturing said, "You go wit you tings?"

I said again, "Huh?"

Betty jumped into the car with Larry Jr. and I finally understood that it would be a great idea if I did the same.

We drove through a small amount of countryside and then into the congested streets of Charlotte Amalie. Traffic seemed to be directed by the use of auto horns. Everywhere we looked we were surrounded by black people. They were walking on the sidewalks, in the street, any where they seemed to choose. The unfamiliar odor of the docks assaulted my nose. This is **Romantic**?

About that time the driver, who had been conducting a guided tour all the way along, of which I understood nothing, said, "De Gran **Ho**tel." Pointing his hand at an old two story, moss covered, building at the end of the street. He stopped in front of the hotel and got out and started unloading our bags. I considered asking if there were another place he could take us, but thought better of it. I was fairly sure we could survive a stay here for at least one night.

Paying the driver and giving a small tip for each bag, we entered the Grand Hotel. The relative darkness and coolness surprised us. We approached the aged, worn front desk, and asked to register. After some small language difficulties we were assigned to a room on the second floor. We trooped up there and made our way to number 216. I produced the large skeleton key on the end of a string attached to a piece of wood and opened the door. Inside was a bed, a dangling light bulb , a stand with a wash basin and a pitcher and not much else. The toilet facility and shower was down the hall. There were screens over the windows and a transom over the door. When both transom and windows were opened a cool breeze flowed through the room. We later learned this was called breeze conditioning.

Opening the windows, we allowed the sounds of the market place to drift up to us. We had a small supply of food with us and the adventurers were just about overwhelmed. We ate a spare supper there and simply remained in our rooms, too exhausted to venture forth. Culture shock had taken its toll. We slept.

The Car Wrangler

     I awoke early the next morning. Sitting in the hotel room with our meager possessions and already hungry, I determined that the first thing to do was to make a list of priorities. What did we need to do to start living on this island? Here is the list after breakfast:

1. Secure our financial ties with our bank in Montana
2. Acquire some mode of transportation
3. find a place to live
4. Report to the Virgin island Department of Education

     The view from our hotel window was of a side street. It didn't really give any idea of the rest of the town. I walked down the hall to the Grand Hotel Balcony. From here, on the second floor, I could see the Main Street. Across the street and down the block not far I spied the Chase Manhattan Bank. Aha! Problem solved.

     Leaving the baggage in the hotel room, we trooped to the Bank. There we met Mrs. Smith, in charge of new accounts. We proceeded to set up a new checking account with $100.00 cash. Then I made arrangements to have one thousand dollars transferred to that account from our bank in Harlowton, Montana. Mrs. Smith said that they conducted these transactions all the time and it wouldn't be a problem. The Montana bank could just wire the money to them and they would credit our account.

     "Great!!! Now, how do we get a car?"

     Mrs. Smith said, "Not a problem. Just go to the car dealer across the street and tell him Mrs. Smith would take care of it. Since you are employed by the Department of Education, you can have the monthly payments simply sent directly to the bank."

     Wonderful!!! So we trooped across the street to the used car lot. The salesman was from the mainland. No problem with the communications. My eyes landed on a wonderful Volkswagen. "Can we take this one for a little test spin?"

"Absolutely!" He smiled. "Just pile on in there and we'll give her a run up the hill and back."

Betty and Larry Jr. hopped in the back and when I realized the salesman was going to drive, I sat down in the passenger seat. He started the car and put it in gear. It was a smooth ride out of the car lot. He turned up a street and suddenly we were going up at a very fast rate. He took several corners left then right then left and we were at the top of the mountain overlooking Charlotte Amalie Harbor. My God! What a beautiful sight. I was having trouble believing we were really there. Now, how am I going to get this car? What will I have to do?

Back at the car lot the salesman was already rubbing his hands together on the way to the little shack he called his office. I leaned back to Betty and Larry Jr. "You guys just stay in the car in the back seat. I'll be back out in just a minute and we can take off."

In his office the lone salesman dropped the keys to the VW casually on the tabletop. He strolled over to the desk area to get the paperwork. I just as casually placed my hand over the top of the keys as I sat down on the table. My hand closed around the keys as he was saying, "Well, we just have a little paperwork here."

I stood and started backing toward the door. "Just see Mrs. Smith over at the Chase Manhattan Bank. Tell her Larry Brasen took the car. She knows all about it."

Objecting, he said, "We usually don't do things this way."

"Not a problem. Not a problem," I said as I exited the shack.

"Hey, what are you doing?" he said.

"Just call Mrs. Smith at the bank," I said, as I opened the car door.

"What the heck is going on?" Betty said from the back seat.

"No problem, no problem." I soothed, putting the key in the ignition.

"Hey, you can't just take the car without signing something!" from the salesman.

"Just call Mrs. Smith. It's all okay," easing the car into gear. "Just wait…" I was in traffic! I made it! I had transportation!

Half a block down the street the traffic stopped moving. One of the few lights on the island had turned red. I applied the brake and with my hand of the gear shift lever, I waited for the traffic to clear. One minute later the way was clear in front of us and I let up on the brake, easing down on the accelerator. NOTHING!!! No movement at all!!! All the way down on the gas. Nothing! Only the sound of the engine racing way to high. Mess with the gear shift lever. Nothing.

Horns starting honking. People who were simply walking down the sidewalk began staring. More Horns!!! Step on the gas. Nothing. Gear shift lever. Nothing. I noticed the people on the sidewalk were beginning to come towards us. They were all black people. "For God's sake, lock the doors," I yelled.

Now the street was filled with white teeth smiling and the whites of eyes staring. They danced, they yelled. Our whole world was seething with black people trying to get the doors open, trying get at us, yelling, touching, feeling. *My God,* I thought. *I've brought my whole family these thousands of miles only to be eaten by cannibals in broad daylight!* Shaking my head, I just gave up and put my hands in the air. The car began to move forward! I grabbed the wheel and applied the brake a little to keep from running over anyone. The crowd began to disperse in front of me. We were going to make it.

Just then I noticed the car salesman in the rear view mirror running toward us at a rapid pace. He was waving some papers in his hand. The traffic was moving along and I turned a corner, put the gas down and left all of them in the dust. **Transportation problem solved.**

Our First Full Day

Our next stop was the Department of Education. We needed to sign in with them and let them know we had arrived. We also were anxious check if any music teaching jobs had opened up. We could make it on just one salary but it would be much better to have two. The Department took up one entire block. There were palm trees blowing in the soft island breeze and hibiscus bushes bloomed near the sidewalk. Once inside, we were ushered into a waiting area and told we would be next to chat with the personnel officer. In just moments we were invited into her office. An attractive native lady came out from behind her desk offering her hand to us. "Wel-**com** to Saint Toe-**maas** Mr. and Mrs. Bra-**sen**. I have been lookin for-**ward** to mee-**tin** you."

We shook hands and exchanged pleasantries for a moment. Then she surprised us by telling us that there was a job opening in the music department at Nazareth Bay High School where Betty was to be teaching reading. If I was still interested in taking a teaching position, I was qualified for the job and could take it right then. It didn't take us long to fill out the remaining paperwork and get our preliminary information. It was at this point that we asked where to sign Larry Jr. up for school. Her answer was not at all what we had anticipated. Through narrowed lids, her eyes roved between Betty, Larry Jr. and me. A slight crease appeared in her forehead indicating she couldn't really understand the question. She said, "Hmmm…Let me seeee…You are not sugges-**tin** that you **in**-tend to place him in an Ie-**lan** school, are you?"

"Well," I picked my way carefully, "What are you suggesting?"

"Oh lord, oh lord, oh lord," She repeated, her head shaking from side to side. "De Is-**land** chil-**dren** would eat dis poor little boy wit de glas**ses** on for lunch and he would not hab a chance. No, no, no. You must take him to de school for de white chil-**dren** here on de is-**lan**. De name of de school is Antil les. Dat is where you mus take de boy."

She even had brochures from Antilles School to hand out. We took one and thanked her. Then she asked us if we had found housing on the island. When we told her we had stayed the night at the Grand Hotel, she had another eye rolling session with herself. She said that there was a nice condominium right on Red Hook Harbor, near our school, which had a vacancy as of that morning. She explained how to find the place and sent us on our way.

The trip to the East Wind Condominiums took us inland past a large supermarket named Grand Union. We stopped there and bought sandwich makings. We were surprised to see beer, wine and hard liquor being sold right along with the groceries. (Sure wasn't that way in Montana.) We were pleased to see that the prices of most goods were quite similar to the stateside prices to which we were accustomed. Back in the VW we were driving on the left side of a paved road that took us through gorgeous tropical views. Everywhere the island was covered with tropical vegetation. Everywhere we looked was a vibrant green. About the time we would forget that we were indeed on an island we would get another view of the sea. Homes built with cement blocks littered the Hillsides. It seemed as if each of the houses belonged, perched there with balconies, looking out over the sea. Occasionally there would be a little cement block one room shanty with a rusted corrugated tin roof. The contrast of such beauty and obvious poverty caught our attention. Soon we arrived at our destination on the east end of the island. It was a new, long, white two story building with coconut palms, hot pink bougainvillea and bright orange hibiscus bushes, banana trees and green manicured lawns. We were thrilled to think we might be able to live in such a beautiful area.

We parked and were shown to a one bedroom, second floor apartment with a view overlooking Red Hook Bay. Stepping out on our balcony that faced the sea, we got our first glimpse of an ocean liner. It was just passing the opening of the bay. Amazing what will take your breath away.

First and last month's rent and a damage deposit set us back one thousand dollars. It didn't take long to spend money here. I was just about out of loot. It was sure a good thing we had made the arrangements with the bank before we started spending. We soon would have to return to the bank and make sure everything was secured with our bank in Montana. Having picked up our meager possessions from the Grand Hotel, we now transferred them to our second floor home. After a quick trip to the nearest department/grocery store where we got additional basic foodstuffs and swim suits for all three of us and a beach blanket we were off to the beach.

It was only a short walk to the white coral beach shining in the sun. We could hear the voices of young people laughing and playing in the water. Both Betty and I had purchased what we considered somewhat immodest bathing attire. My suit was a nylon brief. Betty's suit consisted of very brief pants and a revealing bra—her very first bikini. Larry Junior's was more of a typical kid's suit. Since neither of us had ever been so exposed in public, we were concerned about what other people would think. Because of this, we wore our bathrobes down to the beach over our swim suits. Here we were, flip flopping our way to the beach along a man made coral walkway. Now we were able to see the beach and the people on it. Well, our swim suits were definitely not too revealing. (Whew) We found a spot of beach that was unoccupied and spread our blanket on the coral sand. Now was to be the first test of bravery. Off with the bath robes. We had no idea how white we actually were. The folks next to us said,

"You must be new from the states. You better have some suntan lotion with you. Be sure not stay too long in the sun. Anything over thirty minutes on the first day could result in a nasty burn."

We thanked them and walked down to the water.

It is at this point that I feel it would be proper to tell you that while Betty was a proficient swimmer, I had no idea how to swim. In fact, as we were leaving the Billings, Montana area our good friends, Ted and Bess Adolphsen had shared a special book with me. It was the *Red Cross How To Swim Book.* I had it in my possession there on the beach. I was determined to learn how to swim. We had come all this distance to a wonderful spot on the sea and I was not going to let this opportunity slip past me.

Into the water I walked, Red Cross Swim Book in my right hand. Okay, the water was a little over my knees. This was to be the spot where I changed my world. The temperature of the water was just a little cooler than my skin. It was comfortable considering the afternoon sun was beating down pretty warm. Bending my knees, ever so little, I began to sink into the water. By the time my knees were on the sand the water was up to my shoulders. Holding the book out of the water to prevent getting the pages wet, I allowed myself to slowly sink even lower into the water. Now the water was up to my mouth and my left hand was searching for the sandy bottom. The book had said to take a big breath and then try to relax. You should float. Well, I wasn't floating and as I leaned back my left hand started to sink deeper into the sand. Determined not to allow the pages of the book to get wet, I sank slowly under the water. I had never tried to swim before but I knew there was something wrong with the instructions. Thank God I had taken a big breath before going under. Pushing even deeper with my left hand to get myself righted, I suddenly felt a sharp, painful bite on the skin between my left thumb and forefinger. Of course, that was it for the book. I'm afraid everything got wet at that point if you get my meaning. I know I must not have actually walked on the water getting out of there but you couldn't convince me.

"What in the world is wrong?" This from Betty, "You looked like you were doing pretty good then out you came."

"Something bit me. My hand was in the sand and something bit me."

Our new neighbor informed me that sometimes sand crabs will be at that level and if you bear down on them they will retaliate by pinching you with their claw. "You might try swimming without the book. I think that would help."

"Betty," I said, " you go ahead and try a little swim before we have to leave. You aren't going to believe how salty the water is. It's cool just to taste it. Larry Jr., why don't you and I play in the water at the edge right here. It will be fun."

"Will I get bit by a sand crab?"

Our most informative beach neighbor said, "Very unlikely, Larry Jr. I think you will like it."

We played in the water a while longer and then I noticed that we were starting to get a little red. Back to the apartment we walked, covered as much as possible by our bath robes. Before retiring early we summed up the day. To us it had been one of the most eventful days in our lives. First, we had established our banking institution and made arrangements with our Montana bank.

Second, we had managed to obtain a delightful little automobile (even though the circumstances surrounding its procurement may have been a bit unusual.)

We had signed in at the Department of Education and acquired a second teaching position while obtaining our New Teacher Orientation Information package.

Then, we had driven on the left side of the road all over the island and only lapsed into driving on the right once or twice (mainly when turning corners).

We had gone shopping twice.

We had secured a beautiful tropical apartment with a wonderful view of the sea and access to a great beach.

We had gone for our first "Swim".

The sun set at precisely 6 P.M. When I say "Set" that is what I mean. There were no dust particles in the atmosphere to make for a lingering sunset. One moment the light from the sun was there and the next moment it was gone. Time to turn on the lights.

    We didn't realize it at the time, but we were suffering from intense culture shock. When the human mind is bombarded with new experiences at the rate we were moving, it simply gets overloaded. The reaction is to go to sleep. That is precisely what we did. And so ended our first full day on St. Thomas, USVI.

U S V I School--First Day

      I guess the first day of school is pretty much the same across the world. We started out with a teacher's meeting at 9:30 AM. The district had coffee and doughnuts brought in from Grand Union, the local caterer and general grocery store. (Nice touch) The chairs had been set up in theater style and a podium/microphone were at the front. This was a brand new school. In fact they weren't quite finished with it on this first day. We had all been busy introducing ourselves to each other. It was a nice mix of seasoned Island professionals and new people from State Side. At Ten O'clock sharp Mr. Thomas, the Principal, stood at the microphone and asked all to be seated.

      After a nice welcome he talked for quite some time about grading, discipline, taking attendance, etc. (All the things even the old pros needed to know with this new principal and school.) He had each of us stand up and introduce ourselves and what we taught. Just as I was beginning to think this was going to be a fairly ordinary school year, Mr. Thomas invited the local representative of the teachers union to come to the podium and relay the latest news from the educator's perspective.

      Joe, a tall athletic individual, shook hands with Mr. Thomas and taking the microphone turned to us and began. "As most of you know, the union and the school district are currently at an impasse in this year's negotiations. As such it would be improper for me to talk about it in this setting. I would like to take advantage of this opportunity to invite anyone here, whether a union member of not to attend the general meeting of the union this evening being held at the Charlotte Amalie High School Gym. The meeting is slated to begin at 7 PM and in the event that nothing changes on either side we will be taking a vote as to how to continue on. That makes this a very important meeting for each of us to attend." Smiling, he handed the microphone back to Mr. Thomas.

      After a few more remarks, Mr. Thomas told us we were free to find our mail boxes in the front office and get our class lists, grade books and other material to start school the next day and retire to our rooms and generally get everything ready for tomorrow. Betty and I had agreed to meet outside the main office and go up to our rooms together. The school building was a two story affair up on a hill facing South. Each floor had about twenty classrooms on either side of a long cement walkway. There was a cement Y branching up from the office area to the two openings in the building giving access to that walkway with stairs up to the second floor. There were no air conditioners. The classrooms were fitted with louvered windows which opened for "Breeze Conditioning".

"What do you think about the "Union Thing"? I asked. We had always said we didn't believe in real unions. We had always belonged to the "Professional Organization" (the National Education Association and it's State affiliate) and kind of looked down our noses at "Unions". We would NEVER belong to a UNION!!! (Well, never can be a long time can't it?) I said, "I think I had better go to that meeting this evening and get the lay of the land. Let's find out what we have gotten ourselves into here." Betty agreed to stay home with Larry Jr. and I would go to the meeting. We parted at the top of the stairs and went to our respective rooms. I was excited to meet the rest of the Music Education Staff with whom I would be working. Since I had a little more teaching experience than any of the other Music Teachers, Mr. Thomas asked me to be the Chairman of the Department. I not only said yes but also felt just a little "puffed up" about it all. The staff consisted of:

Don, a French Horn player from the East Coast
Dan, a Trumpet man from the mainland also
John, a Vocalist from the mainland
Roger, a Native Virgin Island Musician
Caroline, a Vocalist from the Mainland
Me, a Brass man & folk guitarist from Montana

Our department consisted of 4 rooms. No chairs or desks or furniture of any kind and no instruments except 2 pianos. There had been a delay in the shipping from Puerto Rico and it would be a couple more days till everything arrived. We held a brainstorming session and went home promising to get together before school in the morning and decide how to proceed with no music for chorus, no books for general music, no instruments for band and so on. I asked if anyone was planning on going to the meeting that evening. No one had decided one way or the other so I told them that I was planning on attending and would report back to them what I discovered.

By then it was lunch time. We all trooped over to Lord Rumbottom's Restaurant for lunch. It was one of my favorite spots on the island to eat. I was rather taken aback when Roger, our Native Virgin Islander, ordered a bottle of Heineken Beer with his sandwich. Man, oh man!!! In Montana that would have been grounds for getting fired. The folks on the island didn't think much about it at all. One of the guys said,

"Hey, isn't that Marlin Perkins, the animal guy, over there?" We all gawked at him and sure enough, there he was. I guess he had been filming his show, Mutual of Omaha's Wild Kingdom, on the island. Huh---How about that? (We let him eat in peace and he returned the favor.)

After puttering around until about 2:30 PM I met Betty and we took off in our unique (stolen) VW to pick Larry Jr. up at the bus drop-off from Antillies School. By the way, we were only given 10 to 15 minutes to vacate the school after 2:30 daily. We got home and went to the beach. After supper I headed into Charlotte Amalie High School for the Union meeting. I arrived just a little before 7 PM when the meeting was scheduled to begin. There were quite a few cars in the school parking lot so I expected a lot of people inside. Upon entering the gym I'll have to say I was amazed at the number of people there. I quit counting at 50 and thought there must have been well over 300 people there. This is a lot of teachers for a small island...Hmmm...

I found one of the folks I met earlier at school and as I started chatting with him, they called for order. We found chairs and sat. A man named Mr. Dennis came to the front and began talking. I must say that I was impressed with his command of public speaking. He talked about how the requests of the Union were reasonable and had the good of the student population and parents at heart, and how the Administration had balked at each item. As he brought up each part of the contract in question and reported the other side's offer, a roar rose up from the crowd that quite honestly scared the living crap out of me. These people were really upset and the longer the meeting continued, the more upset they became. This was beginning to resemble a mob. They had a voice vote and it was decided with a roar to STRIKE!!!. I didn't even believe in unions and I ARE one. I sure as the dickens wasn't going to go against this crowd. Sign me up.

Later at home I made my report to Betty and told her we would be joining the union because as strangers there we needed to choose a side and we are teachers. I didn't want either of us to walk the picket line, because of possible physical harm. We could be part of the planning and support people in the background.

What a first day of School. That was one day out of the way...

FUNDING CYCLE

The strike lasted 3 days. There were few incidents to be noted other than the one time a strike breaker bumped a picket walker with his car. Little damage was done--bruises, scrapes etc. but the union made a big deal out of it. Betty and I didn't walk the picket line. Rather, we were involved with behind the scenes activities--sign making—planning--a newsletter and so on. Just when it was beginning to look like the strike could go on for a long time, it was over. In the meantime, our chairs, desks, instruments and music were delivered to the classrooms. Our first meaningful day with students was spent getting classes ready to start for the year. It wasn't long before most rifts between union and non-union members were healed and we settled down to the business of school as usual.

The following instruments were received from some music company in Puerto Rico:
Flutes 10
Clarinets 10
Oboe 1
Alto Saxes 4
Tenor Saxes 2
Trumpets 10
Horns 4
Trombones 10
Baritone Horns 2
Sousaphones 2
Assorted Percussion equipment

For band music we received a complete set of beginner technique books and one set of a book of famous marches. We didn't get any music for vocalists.

Since we had 3 distinct levels of instrumentalists, we placed them into Beginning, Intermediate and Advanced Band. We divided the beginners into Brass and Woodwind groups and started teaching band. None of the students brought their own instruments to school. The very first thing we had to do was to figure out how to sterilize the mouthpieces. No one on the island had any spray for that so the best we could do was to use a 190 proof alcohol/water bath to dip the mouthpieces. One day Roger informed me that some of the clarinetists were dipping and swallowing the alcohol. (I had been wondering where each batch was disappearing to.) Of course we had to assign one of us to supervise the "Daily Dipping".

For General Music we were supplied with 7th and 8th grade music texts. We used these to teach from along with a generous amount of singing of folk and Calypso songs by ear. I typed up the lyrics and handed them out and taught harmonies by ear. We also made great use of the singing of rounds.

About a month into the school year Mr. Thomas, at a staff meeting of Department Chairmen, gave us an assignment we all would find time consuming and important. We were assigned to submit a budget for any supplemental items that had not been covered in the initial order for the school supplies. I spent a weekend at home collating our music staff's requests and trying to find suppliers and prices for everything. (No beach for me that weekend) Bright and early Monday morning I handed in a file folder with ten or more pages of orders in it. Mr. Thomas gave it a glance and said, "Mistah Braz, would you be good enough to go through these items and mark the ones you cannot do without during this school year? Then hand it back in to me."

I kind of thought that was what I had already done but I said I would do as he asked. After going through the list I handed back in about half of the original list. I asked when we could expect the items we had ordered and was told it could be some time because the orders had to be put out to bid and because of our remote location it could take some time for the supplies to arrive from the mainland or Puerto Rico by boat. We all settled in to wait for the materials to arrive and in the meantime went about our daily schedules teaching music.

After handing in the requisitions I waited for some time to hear from anyone about the disposition of the orders. Then I waited some more. After a month or two I decided to ask Mr. Thomas about the orders. He said he turned them in to the Department of Education and if I needed to know how they were being handled, I would need to check in with the Department downtown. So I made the appropriate arrangements and traveled to the Offices in Charlotte Amalie. When I asked the person in charge of ordering supplies, he just shook his head and said I was welcome to look in the ordering room. He indicated a door and said I could find my requisitions in the Nazareth Bay stacks. The door opened into a room the size of a football field filled with tables stacked 2 to 3 feet high with requisitions. God only knew how long they had been collecting dust. There was just barely room to move between the tables. My "Helper" indicated a specific table and said he thought that my "Stuff" might be somewhere on it.

After about an hour of sifting through the stacks of broken promises and dreams I found my small set of "Reqs". I took them to the man in charge and asked if there were any chance he could help me with them. He said they had run out of money for the year and they would be considered for the next fiscal unit. I asked permission to take them with me and he was happy to let them go. When I returned to the school we had a Music Department meeting in our converted janitor's room I called the office. We all decided that if we were to get any of the material we ordered, we would need to fund it ourselves. That was the birth of the "Incredible World's Finest Chocolate Fund Raiser of Nazareth Bay Junior/Senior High".

We discovered the "World's Finest Chocolate" Fund Raising Company had an outlet on Puerto Rico, only a day away by delivery boat. The representative came and talked to all the music classes. That was everyone in the seventh, eighth and most of the ninth grades. We figured how many we thought each student would sell on average and did the math. We placed our order and waited for the shipment of candy to come in. We didn't take into consideration that each of these great salesmen and women would have to taste their wares before selling to friends, neighbors, anyone who liked chocolate and their uncle. The day the shipment came in we put it under lock and key with the famous "Alcohol Dip". It took up most of one practice room, measuring about four cubic feet. (A monstrous pile of chocolate bars.) After the second day of our ten day sale we were out of chocolate. A quick phone call over to Puerto Rico and 2 days later we were back in business. I was keeping the receipts from the sale in my locked filing cabinet during the day in my janitor/music office. I took the money home with me at night and put it in a special bank account. On Friday of the second week of the sale (last day) we found the door to the office had been pryed open and so had the filing cabinet even though the door and the drawer had been locked. Nothing had been taken but someone sure had their eyes on the project. We used the funds to purchase music and other necessities throughout the year and into the next year. It seemed as though the alcohol disinfectant always needed replacement...(Just sayin')

Carnival—Pronounced Car-nee-vaal

Many of the Caribbean Islands and nations in the Southern Hemisphere celebrate Carnival. From New Orleans (Marti Gras) to Rio the folks seem to go just a little crazy at that time of year. For you Trekies out there I believe Spock would refer to it as Amok. It is "The" pre-lent festival. People dress up or down as they desire in the most outlandish and beautiful colors beyond imagining; drink alcoholic beverages of their choice and size (usually large and rummy); cavort through the streets dancing as they go from no place to no place. And then there is the music-The ubiquitous beat of the islands-long long quick – long long quick – over and over again. Dotted quarter, dotted quarter, quarter—repeat… Every home, every store, every eatery, every bar, every boat, every coconut palm, at the docks, in the church, Bluebeard's Castle, the ninty-nine steps, all invasive, all inclusive, omnipresent. Not just one day or even one week. The preparations begin much earlier. Floats being constructed; songs being written; costumes being decided upon and tailored; All in the context of rum consumption and ever escalating emotions. Try teaching Junior High School in that atmosphere.

The actual celebration itself lasted one week during which there were a variety of activities all over the island. The children as well as the adults attended many of these late night excursions and it certainly showed the next day as the kids came to school. Some people thought that we might just as well dismiss school for that week for all the good we were doing. On the other hand, how would we prepare for our participation on the final Saturday event if we were not in school? So…school it was. Our school was going to be celebrating with all the others. The big problem for our Music Department was that we still didn't have much of a band truly ready for the big parade. I had purchased a large number of L.P.s of Island Music. After listening to many songs on record I caught on to that Calypso beat that coursed through the measures song after song. I decided I could write a Carnival Parade song just for our school. I gave the Sousaphone and Baritone Horns a bass line that followed the chord pattern. Then I gave the upper brass and woodwinds triads to play following that basic island beat. I found it totally unnecessary to write a drum part. The percussion section was far better at improvising their part than anything I might write. I wrote it all out in longhand (copy machines were very limited in their functions) and handed it out to the advanced band. I called the piece **"Fungi Boombala Buckup, 1972"**. It was an instant hit with all. Within a couple of days the band was parading through the hall playing it by memory or by ear. (I didn't care which) One teacher asked me, "What is the melody to that song?" I had to reply, "Oh, did you think there was a melody?"

    Mister Thomas gave me a glowing evaluation for taking part in the parade and creating my own little *masterpiece* for the school's part in the festivities.

Rupert

On Wednesday of the Carnival week Betty and I arrived a little early at the school as was my custom. I parked "de Bug" close to my office on the ground floor of classrooms and Betty and I got out to go to work.

Betty had previously introduced me to her self appointed hall walking guard. Of course, no guard was needed, but "Mista King" liked meeting us and "guarding" Betty to her room. He was a large down-islander and I thought the main reason he got up and went to school was to meet Betty and Me at the West end and walk her to her classroom. When introduced I asked him what his first name was. He replied, "King." To that I asked, "You mean your name is King King?" With a smile of surprise and pleasure he nodded, "King King. Very good name." As we walked down the breezeway hall we were greeted by two very excited students of mine. Running up to us they yelled out, "Mista Braaz, Mista Braaz. You did see Ru**pert**, mah son?"

"Whoa, whoa. What's this about? Did you say Ru**pert**? Our trumpet player?"

"Ru**pert**, yah Ru**pert**. Rupert did hit de canejuice baad, mah son! He did drink de whole **quaat**, mah son, an he does be runnin like cra**zee**! Bum**pee** do be lookin fo he now. Big trou**bol**, **big** trou**bol**."

Mr. Thomas, our school principal, was physically a little stout. He carried a lot of his weight on the back of his hips. The students gave him the nickname "Bumpee". I'm fairly certain that he wasn't called that to his face but everyone seemed to think the moniker was just a little funny and I for one wouldn't have attempted to correct the kids for using it.

"Well, keep your eyes open and if you see him send him up to me," I said, hoping that it didn't happen.

Betty's hall walking guard, King King, was waiting at the door to my classroom. They started down the hall and I went into my room to get ready for the day's activities. I no sooner laid my books on my desk than the door crashed open and three students came rushing in. Breathlessly —"Mistaa Braaz, Mistaa Braaz, Rupert com**in**. Rupert com**in**. He Baad, mah son! Soo baad!" Heads shaking hopelessly.

"Where is he?" I was getting worried.

"He upstair com**in** down now!"

"Is he com**in** here? I sounded like an islander.

"De boy wit de hair say to he come to you like you said."

What the heck am I going to do now? Turn him in? I don't think so. In Montana, where I came from, there are rules to be followed in cases like this and if you don't follow them you would lose your job. I didn't feel like loosing my job, that was for sure.

At that exact moment I ran out of options. The door nearly flew off the hinges as Rupert came tearing into the room. He was singing a calypso song at the top of his voice and running around the perimeter of the room. He ran so fast that his feet didn't even touch the floor. He was running on the walls. This kid was fast.

I tried to get his attention but he was in his own world. Running, singing, yelling, beating the drum when he ran past it and strumming the louvers on the windows. Then in a move that required three to five seconds, he curled up in a ball in a corner and went to sleep. I checked for a pulse. Yep, he was alive...

The door to the hallway burst open and "de boy wit de long hair" ran right up to me. Out of breath he cried, "Bum**pee** Com**in**, Bum**pee** Com**in**. Oh, Mistaa Braaz, Bum**pee** Comin. What you do do now?"

"What? Here? Now? Oh, God!!! Where is he right now?" I shouted.

"He dawng de hall. Jus halfway. But he com**in**!"

"Maybe I can bluff my way through this and keep my job", I thought. I stepped to the door and entered the hall. There was my boss, Mr. Thomas, two doors away.

"Ah, Mistaa Braa**zin**. Just the man I'm look**in** for. I've had a report about a student named Ru**pert**. Do you know any students named Ru**pert** Mistaa Braa**zin**?"

"Ah, Rupert. Rupert. Let's see. Would that possibly be Rupert the trumpet player?" stalling for time.

"I do believe that might just be the Rupert I'm looking for", he replied politely. "Have you seen him today?"

"Today, Today. You mean like earlier today don't you? I believe I have seen him today. Yes I think so."

Mr. Thomas was an expert at digging out the truth. "When would you estimate that to have been, Mistaa Braa**zin**?"

Starting to give up I said, "Just a few minutes ago I may have seen him briefly."

Digging ever deeper, "Mistaa Braazin, Could I ask you where this possible sighting might have taken place?"

"In my room, Mr. Thomas. He is in there now, sleeping off an unfortunate occurrence that happened this morning. He is not bothering anyone where he is."

Oh, crud!!! Here it comes!!!

Mr. Thomas looked at me for some time. I was silent, waiting for the axe to fall. I deserved it and I knew it. Stroking his chin, as he sometimes did, he said, "You know, Mistaa Braazin, I think you might just make a great teacher here in de Islands. We shook hands and he turned and walked back down the hall.

Later that day as I was walking down the sidewalk to the administration offices to check my mail, one of my students named Charles, caught up with me and fell in step. He had witnessed the "Rupert Affair" and he said to me as we made our way, "Mistaa Braaz. Me Blackie...You Whitey...If we cut, our blood be RED! You Black inside my son!!! You and me, we Black!!!"

It caught me off guard. A sharp intake of breath. Voice a little shaky, "Thanks, Charles. That's the nicest thing I've heard in a long time."

Sailing With Jack

I had always been mildly interested in sail boats. It seemed a mystery to me how the boats in a strong wind would tip way over but not upset. I knew it had something to do with the weighted keel but I hadn't studied the phenomenon. Since I had never learned to swim, it was very unlikely I would ever be on a sail boat. We had been in Saint Thomas, teaching at Nazareth Bay High School for a few weeks, when a new acquaintance named Jack Beaver, a math teacher there, mentioned he was living on a 26 foot Sloop he had sailed down from Chesapeake Bay arriving just in time for the start of school. It wasn't long before Betty, Larry Jr, and I found ourselves going for a day sail with Jack as the Master Instructor.

Jack had been a drill instructor in the United States Marine Corps. Once we got on the boat, the old DI came out in full force. In no uncertain terms, he was the **captain** of the ship. He would give the orders and it would be our duty to obey, without questioning ASAP. He made it clear that the hesitation of a second could make the difference between life and death on the water. We were suitably impressed. He gave us a ten minute lecture concerning the proper nomenclature of all the lines, sheets, pulleys, cleats, mast, boom, sail, jib etc. (There would me no such thing as a **rope** on this ship. Ropes are for cowboys.)

We spent a nice day on the water, sailing up Drakes Passage on the North side of Saint John. We then took a tack that brought us into Roadtown Harbor on Tortola, BVI. We moored the boat and walked up the street to a favorite ice cream parlor where we all had ice cream cones. Jack claimed they helped prevent sea sickness. By the time we arrived back at Vessup Bay and home, we were hooked.

One thing I noticed after getting off the boat...my legs had forgotten how to walk. I stepped onto the pier and nearly fell right into the water. I was sure the pier wasn't moving side to side and fore and aft but I was totally unable to convince my legs of that. I grabbed hold of Betty with one hand and Larry Jr. with the other, and we wobbled toward Lord Rumbottoms cafe there at Red Hook. "You know what, Betty, I think we better get in our little VW and beat feet for home." Yes, even with that, WE WERE HOOKED!

A couple weeks went by during which we were busy teaching, swimming, eating new food, and getting accustomed to Larry Junior's school schedule which included a 20 mile round trip every morning to get him to the Antilles School. Everywhere we looked we saw sail boats and we tried to imagine sailing them. It was becoming an overwhelming passion. On a Thursday afternoon after school, Jack Beaver asked us if we would like to make an overnight sail with him up to the little Island of Jost Van Dyke. Of course we agreed and so on Saturday morning we met Jack at the pier at Red Hook Harbor Marina. As I recall, his was a 26 foot Columbia sloop rig. Plenty of room for all four of us.

    We hoisted the sail, then the jib, and just let them luff. Then we cast off the mooring line and pulled in the sails. They caught the ever present breeze and we were off. Jack's sailing expertise brought us right through the moored boats and into the open water without a problem. We sailed over to the North side of Saint John and anchored in Trunk Bay. We went ashore and had lunch on the beach. The island of Saint John is almost entirely a National Park. It was donated by the Rockefeller family years ago. There are several ruins of sugar plantations available for investigating. Our heads were filled with pictures of life in the far past with slaves, plantation managers, and ships sailing in and out from far reaching points all over the world.

    That afternoon we set sail for the island of Jost Van Dyke. We were beginning to get the feel of the sails catching the wind as we hoisted the anchor and tightened the sheets. It is always exciting to feel the boat moving through the water using only the power of the wind. By the time we sailed into the harbor at Jost Van Dyke, the sun was getting low in the west. It is amazing how quickly the sun goes down in the islands. Because there is not anything in the air to catch the sun's rays, there is little or no lingering dusk. One moment the sun is there and the next it is total night time.

    Jack had radioed in to Foxy's restaurant and reserved four places for us for supper. We had no idea what eating at Foxy's would entail. When we got to the establishment, we were surprised to find only picnic tables on the sandy beach. Several others who's boats were also moored in the harbor had already arrived and were seated on the benches at the tables. We were told to find a place with someone who was at a table and we would be served family style. After introducing ourselves to the others Foxy came to our table and introduced himself to each person individually. He made a point of getting each of our names, including Larry Jr., and after all the introductions were finished he went to each of the other tables and repeated the procedure. The Langoustine dinners complete with corn on the cob dripping with butter, green salad, rice and beverages were served. (Longoustine is warm water lobster. They lack the large claw but do have large antennae who's meat is edible.) During the meal, Foxy came and while accompanying himself with the guitar, he sang a calypso song of his own crafting which included a verse about every single person there using their names and there must have been 25 to 30 folks there. I know he didn't write the names down as he met everyone. He has trained his memory... I wonder if he is still there doing the same thing. Following supper we returned to the boat and bunked in for the night. Once you become accustomed to the rocking motion of the water, it just kind of lulls you to sleep. Prior to drifting off to never never land, Jack treated us to a nightcap named after his sloop. It was named The Sorcierre. The drink consisted of Tang powdered orange juice, some water, (not much) and of course Virgin Island Rum.

  The next day, Sunday, we sailed down the Northwest coast of Tortola and then returned home to Jessup Bay where Jack moored his sloop. When we got back to our apartment, my whole world was pulsing with each heart beat. While I wasn't sick, I was about as close to it as I had been during the two days at sea. We all experienced the feeling of the pulse of the waves while back on land. After simply sitting down and resting all three of us recovered. That overnighter sealed our fate. We began looking in earnest for a sloop of our own.

OUR FIRST SAIL ON THE "BAG END"

We had several names picked out for the new addition to our family. Our sloop... we finally chose to name her "The Bag End" after the home of Bilbo Baggins of "The Hobbitt" fame. We spent several days taking our dingy we named "Bzzzt", out to the Bag End just getting acquainted with her. She was a fine little 25 foot sloop rig built in the Netherlands by the Folker company. I'm sure there are a bunch of details I should include here about beam and draft and weight of the keel etc. but that all eludes me. There was a nice cabin with benches and a table that could make into beds to accommodate two couples and a berth in the forecastle for one person. There was a head that actually flushed sea water. She also had a galley on a gimbal. (We could have soup on and not spill a drop.)

Today was the big day for the first sail. Since she was equipped with a small Johnson outboard, getting out of the marina was a snap. We simply started up the engine, let go the mooring line, and putt-putted our way through the other boats out into open water dragging "Bzzzt" on a medium line. If I had known at the time what was about to happen, I would have gone further out to sea before attempting to set the sails. When we were what appeared to be a safe distance from the Eastern shore of St. Thomas, we killed the engine and went about hoisting the jib and the mainsail. I didn't take into account the ever present Easterly wind blowing us toward the shore. Since we hadn't practiced it at anchor, there were a couple of hitches in our get-alongs for which we were not fully prepared. Half way up the mast our jib got fouled in the jib track. As we were all trying to work on the jib, we didn't notice that the Easterly was pushing us gradually toward the shore where the waves were crashing on boulders. We got the jib up and started hoisting the mainsail when I became aware of the sound of a tremendous crashing of waves on the rocks. I glanced over at the shore and was shocked to see the white foam being thrown into the air. My God!!! I could even distinguish the plant life growing on the huge volcanic boulders. I started pulling the starter on the outboard motor and of course the miserable thing wouldn't catch. We were just about a block away from the shore. Just as we were about die in the boating accident of the year, the engine started and we were able to guide the Bag End out of harms way into deep water.

With our sails set and the outboard off we began a Northeasterly tack intending to eventually anchor at Caneel Bay Plantation. Caneel Bay was famous for their Sunday morning smorgasbord brunch. It looked to be about a block long on both sides of the tables set out in the beautiful sunshine. When we had gone some distance, I said, "Well, it's about time to take a different tack. Betty, you get ready to let go of the main sheet on this side and get under the boom as we cross the wind and bring the sheet in on the other side. Larry, be sure to keep your head down when the boom comes across. Everybody ready? HARD ALEE!" With that I gave the stick tiller a push all the way away from me and the Bag End moved right across the wind as Betty began pulling in the sheet on the other side. She brought it in tight and clamped off just as Jack had taught us. It was a perfect tack. Of course I had misjudged the length of the tack and we had to do the procedure several times to finally get into the Caneel Bay Plantation mooring area.

After a grand Brunch at the Plantation, we dingied back to the Bag End and climbed aboard. On the way back home we got to practice one of the most difficult point of sailing called wing and wing. With the wind exactly at our back we let the mainsail out on the port and the jib out on the starboard. The thing that's difficult is to keep the boat steady so you don't lose the wind in the sails. The potentially dangerous circumstance could be the main sail jibing; that is accidentally having it switch sides which almost always occurs with a great force. People have had equipment break in an accidental jibe. We came about at what we now knew as a respectful distance from the home mooring spot and brought down the jib and the main. We entered Red Hook Harbor under the power of the outboard. We came down past our mooring buoy, came about, cut the motor, and drifted right up to the buoy. Betty and Larry Jr. caught the buoy with the hook and they tied us to the mooring anchor in Jessup bay, just across from Lord Rumbottoms Restaurant. We piled in the "Bzzzt", dingied to the pier, got out, jumped in our little VW and went directly home. Man oh man, did we ever think we were something. Mission accomplished!!!

Jim And Shirley Duderstadt's Playhouse

Early in that first year I met a fellow teacher named Jim Duderstadt. He was part of the English Department as I recall. He sought me out as a music teacher since he was interested in music and drama as well as language. He told me he held plays at his home on the island where he had created an amateur theater. He asked if Betty and I had any interest in being cast in his next production, "Dirty Work At The Crossroads". Since I had been involved in drama during High School and College, and Betty had been active in theater in High School, we were signed up as cast and crew on the spot.

One of our Music Department members, John, had a great voice and he agreed to play the Hero. This was a typical Melodrama. There was a lot of singing and overacting taking place and I got to be the Villain. Betty was cast as the "Mother of the Fair Maiden" and away we went. We gave the show to several audiences to much acclaim. Betty was cast as the "Telephone Operator" in the next play which featured the murder of a bedridden invalid who overheard a telephone call planning her own demise. Scary stuff!!!

Through the years we took part in several plays with Jim and his wife Shirley. It was always a highlight of the Winter Season on the island.

Moving to our two bedroom home

Toward the end of the first school year, which was similar to the dates we were accustomed to in Montana, our school librarian, Rose, told us about a two bedroom home available to rent on an annual basis. Since we were renting the condo apartment on the same kind of yearly basis, we wanted to have the contracts run out and start as close as we could. After looking at the new rental property with a large glassed/screened in living room and a utility kitchen, two bedrooms, sitting on top of a self contained cistern fed by rain water from our own roof, and a great view of Red Hook Bay and our 25 foot sloop, "The Bag End", we were ready. All we had to do was come up with the first and last month rent and a security deposit. We then had to tell our present landlord we were moving at the end of the lease. We had experienced a little disagreement with the Eastwind owner/leaser about our water usage. Since it was on a meter and I had taken down the original reading, we didn't have anything to worry about. We were happy to leave there even if it had been our introductory living space on the island. With a little help from our friends, we were moved in short order and relaxing with a little help from Mr. Heineken.

Cane Juice

    A beautiful 4 day weekend. Weekends in the islands are calculated for maximum leisure time activities. The folks in charge of planning holidays tried to make as many 4 day weekends as possible. You would have a 4 day week, a 4 day weekend, and another 4 day week. We loved it for boating. We could provision ahead for the 3 and a half day vacation and just spend the Friday, Saturday and Sunday nights on the "Bag End" and sail home on Monday morning.

    This day was special because we had guests aboard. Roger and Carolyn, two members of my music teaching staff had come along for the holiday. We had planned to meet our boating friends, John in his boat and Dan in his boat at Cane Garden Bay, Tortola, BVI . Since both of them were also staff members in our music department at Nazareth Bay High School we planned to anchor together for a festive evening of food, drinks of preference, and singing and guitar playing.

    We started out from St. John early in the morning and set sail on a tack for Cane Garden. It was generally a Northerly sail so we could make great time setting the 25 footer on a beam reach using the wind out of the east. Around noon as we neared the wide mouth of the harbor, we sighted a sail off in the North. Using the fine field glasses, a gift from our Montana friends, Ted and Bess, we made out the sail and shape of John's boat. Then we also made out the shape of Dan's boat coming in from the West. It looked like our plans were coming to together.

    We were the first to enter the wide harbor and we tacked back and forth a couple times, then when near the beach we pointed into the wind and let the sail luff. When we stopped our forward movement and started to drift back on the wind, we dropped anchor in the white coral sand and when the line came to about a seven to one angle we just tied her off and let the boat pull the Danforth anchor down into the sand and we were moored.

    In short order both Dan and John pulled up fairly close by and anchored. We then threw lines to each other and pulling the lines got our bumpers to touch on the sides of the boats and we had a three boat flotilla. We could easily walk/jump from one boat to another. Over on the beach was what appeared to be a little food shack. We all dingied over to the beach and pulling our dingies ashore we went as a group towards the little shack. We had only gone a short distance when a wizened little old black man with no front teeth and a walking stick approached. He said he could take us to a very special place if we would like. "Not far, not far", He said in his Caribbean English. We all looked at each other and for some unknown reason agreed to allow this strange little man to guide us into the dense "Bush" as the jungle overgrowth was known. There was a fairly distinct path to follow and we hiked back into the bush the distance of a couple of city blocks. We came to a clearing and there was a dilapidated building of weathered wood and a bunch of metal gears and machinery none of us recognized. We asked him what it was and he said, "De Cane, de Cane!" Gesticulating toward the mountain we were at the foot of he said, "Cane Garden, Cane Garden!!!"

The mountain had been made into cane fields much the same as you might see rice paddies in Asia. He made it clear that the cane grew on the mountain and when harvested was brought to this location to be ground up with the machines we saw there. Then the juice was allowed to ferment and when ready was distilled into rum. He then creaked open the door to the shack and motioned everyone inside. Once there we became aware of a large round metal tub 6 to 8 feet across and five or six feet deep. It was filled to near the top with a clear liquid. "What's in the tub?" I asked.

"AH, CANE JUICE, CANE JUICE!" he said. "Want to try?" Hesitantly, I said, "After you!" He blew the dust out of an old tin cup and reached in and scooped out a meaningful amount of the rum. Sipping it with reverence, He repeated himself, "Ah, Cane Juice!" I received the cup and taking a deep breath, took a mouthful. It was like the finest Cognac I had ever tasted. Everyone who wanted to got to taste this rare treat. I asked him if I could buy a bottle of this cane juice. He grabbed an empty, dirty Canada Dry Ginger Ale bottle off the shelf. Blowing out the cobwebs he produced a rubber hose and siphoned the bottle full. (He didn't neglect the beginning and ending drops of the siphoning process.) "How much?" I asked. "Fifty cents", was his reply. (I doubt to this day that he had a right to do any of the things he had done that day with us.)

"Well, time for us to get back to the beach. Thanks for the tour and the Cane Juice," I said. We all exited the building and looking around were amazed to find the little "Cane Juice Man" had disappeared. Finding the path we had walked, we started back. There was just room to walk single file. Half way to the beach we came upon a giant black guy working on an upturned boat. I was smoking a Camel cigarette at the time and this 400 pound giant stood and walked straight toward our little group. He had his right hand in a gunny sack. In his left hand he held a claw hammer. The giant growled, "You got smokes?" "Sure", I stammered. "Here, You want one?"

"Ah, American smokes. Very good."

I handed him a cigarette offering a light.

Standing up to his tallest and expanding his huge chest he withdrew his hand from the gunny sack and in it gleamed a machete which he waved in the air making fierce slicing motions. He roared through his yellow teeth, "You know what this is?"

In a supreme effort of bowel control and breath support I replied calmly, "Cut Lash"! (I happened to know that is what the Virgin Islanders called a Machete.)

Slowly lowering the deadly instrument he whispered, "You say CUT LASH? Where you from?"

"We teach music over on Saint Thomas," I said.

"Can I have more smokes?"

"You Bet"!

Throwing him the remainder of the pack we beat a quick retreat to the beach and back to our boats.

Every time I tell this story people ask me what I thought he was really doing. I tell them, as I am telling you now, that I have no idea, but I know he wound up with my smokes and we wound up with our heads (and a bottle of Cane Juice).

Lobster From "Scratch"

Something in the core of my being loves to do things from "scratch". For example, I find it more satisfying to catch trout on a fly I tied myself as opposed to a fly I buy at a store. I find I prefer drinking wine I made myself as opposed to wine I buy. Well, here we are living in the Islands and I think it would be better to cook lobster on our stove than to buy lobster precooked. This in mind, we troupe down to the local fish monger just as the boats are coming in to buy two fresh lobsters to take home and cook. We carried them home in a small cloth sack filled with ice to keep them alive. (They did kick a bit. They have a very strong tail you know.) Since these were langoustine (warm water lobster) they had very long antennas and didn't have a large claw to worry about. At the time we thought the trade-off was just fine. We did have some things to learn!
We had read up extensively on the subject of boiling lobsters, and found a variety of opinions depending on the cook book we read. We read "The Joy of Cooking", "Betty Crocker", "Better Homes and Gardens" and others. Although it seemed to be to be the most humane to get the water boiling first then just drop the guy in so his senses are overcome as rapidly as possible, the predominate method seemed to be to place the lobster in tepid water and then heat it gradually. We always heard, "If you drop a frog in boiling water, he'll jump right out. Put the frog in warm water and heat it gradually, by the time he realizes he's in trouble, its too hot and he's too late." We decided on the latter method. (Although we had nothing to do with amphibians.)

With the water in a large covered aluminum pot we drew the lobsters from the sack. "Yeeouch! That shell is sharp! Am I bleeding?"

Betty said, "Get a glove or something. Here, use this bathrobe."

"Bathrobe...are you joking? What's my bathrobe doing in the kitchen?"

"We left all our gloves in Montana."

"Oh, yeah!"

"Help get the lid on the pot!"

"Their antennas are too long. They won't fit in."

"Break 'em off!"

"My God, you can't do that, it would be cruelty to animals."

"What do you call what we ARE doing?"

"Here, can you bend them around a little?"

"Get the lid on quick!"

With that we got the lid on and lit the stove under them. We adjourned to the living room. Briefly we heard a racket like the devil was loose in the kitchen. Tearing around the corner we caught the "Pot from Hell" just as it was about to jump off the stove. The lid was off and one of the lobsters was on his way out. "Down, Down, you wild crustacean!!!" as I beat it with my shoe. The noise of their legs and tails flopping against the pot...Oh, my God!!! "Tie the lid on and let's get the hell out of here for a bit."

"What do we use to tie it down?"

"Here, use the belt from your bath robe."

"Wow!"

"Amen!"

We left the pot jumping and whacking on the stove. Outside, on the veranda, the air was the same balmy breeze we had come to expect and love. "What are we going to do"? I asked.

Well, one thing for sure, we are NOT going to tell anyone about this whole thing. I just feel kind of sick about it",Betty said.

Larry Jr. asked, "Are we still gonna try to eat 'em?"

I finished up my unfiltered Camel cigarette and said, "I think we could go in now."

The lobsters were a nice bright pink and done to a tee. Drawn garlic butter dripping from our elbows, Larry Jr., Betty and I agreed that next time we would go ahead and use lobsters someone else had done in. Let them start from "Scratch", and we'll take if from there.

SOUR SOP BYE BYE

Moving from one creative solution to the next, we arrived at a kind of pattern of "Group Therapy" for the members of the Music Department at Nazareth Bay High School. The last Friday of every month we would meet at our place for some R & R. Betty would bake bread, we would get a couple of six packs of beer, and we would just kick back, relax and make some folk music (Kingston Trio, Harry Bellefonte and Peter, Paul and Mary were still enjoyed by most of us). There was always a lot of "My God, I had a kid do this!" followed by "Well, how about that (insert student's name)? Any of you have him in class? He came to band with a smile like a bear with a rotten rack of lamb. If I didn't know better, I would say he had been smoking something over lunch."

"They say they have a regular den made out in the bush West of the school. I'm sure not going out there to find out."

"Hey, could you toss me another beer? Somebody musta drunk mine."

"Yah, I hate it when that happens. Here...."

"Hey, Roger. Have you ever tried Sour Sop Tea?"

"I heard it can really relax you."

"God, that bread sure smells good. It must be just about done, isn't it, Betty?"

"I like mine with cold, hard butter on it. Melts in your mouth."

"Any of you guys try Onion Kukken (I'm asking John to forgive me for the spelling) and new wine?"

"What is Sour Sop Tea, Roger?"

"Oh, we call it many names but it is generally called "Bush Tea". You take the leaves of special plants and boil them in water until it gets some color to it and then you let it cool a bit and drink it down. Relaxes you, you know?"

"Well, they told us that that tree right out there is a Sour Sop. I suppose we could pick some leaves and make the tea. What does it taste like and what is in it?"

"I've never tried it, so I don't know."

Outside now---

"Do you take leaves right off the tree or do you use ones that have fallen on the ground?"

"I think you take them right off the tree. Let's see..."
"Here, I got some."
"Me too."
"How many does it take?"
"I don't know, but for this many people I imagine it will take quite a few."
"ARE WE REALLY GONNA DO THIS?"
"Well, what the heck. Did you ever hear of anyone dying from Bush Tea?"

It wasn't long before the water was boiling in our "Lobster Pot". In went the leaves and we all watched, fascinated with what we were doing. Sure enough, the water started turning a kind of dirty green. We turned off the heat and let it cool, poured out a shot glass of "Tea" for everyone and we said, "Through the lips, over the gums, look out stomach, here it comes." Not surprisingly, It tasted dirty green. We all looked at each other. Waiting... Nothing...

We went back into the living room and sat down. We were just quietly chatting and then we all started waking up a couple of hours later. What the...

EPILOGUE

Several months later, we had taken Larry Jr. to the doctor for a persistent cough. I asked the Doctor what is in Sour Sop leaves. The answer.....Phenobarbital.....

Quite a nice sleep-in. Never repeated it to this day.

LIFE IN THE U.S.V.I.

The following memories are each less than a short story, but together paint a sort of vignette of our life style in the Virgin Islands. It is my hope you can kind of get the picture.

Roger, Heineken, Anchovies, Biscuit & The Giant Iguana

Betty and I had been out driving around the island. We had been up towards the top of the mountain on what they called the French side. The story we were told was that during the history of the island the French had occupied it at one time. They had made homes on the North side and then when some other country, probably the Dutch, had taken it over, some of the French folks had stayed on. We heard they spoke a sort of rudimentary folk french and didn't intermingle with the rest of the Islanders. We had stopped into a little hutch with a small pool table and played a couple games. We were nearly back home when the car ran out of gas. **Damn!!!** Nothing to do but walk up the hill to where we lived and see if we could get any help from any friends. Roger came through. He came over to our place and said he could give me a ride to the gas station down in Nadir and even had a gas can we could use.

On our way back with the gas he suggested we stop at a shack where they sold beer and biscuits. I told him I would love to give it a try. We parked on the roadside and strolled into the little store. The sound of a television was audible in the back room. We cleared our throats and waited. The sound from the back room was suddenly alarmingly loud. Two women were yelling at the top of their voices. "Donn do **eet** mah la-**dee**. Oh, Gawd!!! He Baad me son!!! He ve-**ry** Baad!!!"

"What the hell is going on, Roger?"

"The ladies are just watching the soaps."

About that time one of the gals came out to the counter they had rigged up in the front of the shop. "My man bet-**tah** not do daat to me. No sir." She pounded the makeshift board. I stepped back a bit. Roger simply said, "How is your day goin, my dear?" She was at once congenial. I learned the lesson right there. Do not treat people behind the counter as though they are some sort of machine, there for your sole convenience. These are people and they demand they be treated as such.

"Can I help you?

"We would like to have two Heinekens, some biscuit and a tin of anchovies. And do you have any hot sauce to go with that?" He plunked some money down and then proceeded to show me how to really enjoy a cool beer. What he called "Biscuit" I would have called large soda crackers. He opened the fish. "Lord Roger, do you eat those little guys bones and all?" He sprinkled the hot sauce on them, popped them in his mouth and washed it all down with the beer. I haven't been able to do it to this day.

We got an extra beer for the road and motivated on down the road. As we were just finishing off our second beer in as many minutes, Roger suddenly came to a complete stop. I looked up the road and to my amazement saw a four or five foot iguana sunning itself on the road. "Holy crap, Roger. What the hell is that?"

"That is a very large iguana."

"Wow. I wonder if I can touch it?"

"Oh, No!!! Don't touch it!!!"

Opening the car door, I said, "I wonder if its tail would come off if I grabbed it." Stepping out of the car, wobbling a little, I started toward the beautiful thing shining in the sun. At that point it did its "push-up thing" and I could see how really large it was. As I was struggling to rethink my original decision, the iguana ran away into the bush so fast that if it had decided to run at me, I know I would never have been able to get back in the car fast enough.

Roger later told me that they can lash you with their tails and secrete a venom at the base of their tail that can make your skin fall off or some other dreadful biological disaster. When I saw the speed of that thing, I knew that Roger knew best.

Cafe Brittany

There was one restaurant we particularly enjoyed. It was named Cafe Brittany. We called ahead and made reservations for the three of us. When we arrived there were little match boxes with our names on them. (Nice touch) We loved steak and lobster. One time we ordered Escargot. The snails came in the shell with a little fork to twist them out. Dunk them in garlic butter and down they go. (We only ordered them once) I believe my favorite was French Onion Soup, covered with cheese and floating a piece of toast on top.

The Oar House

We ate out several times at the Oar House. They served beer by the pitcher and Chili Rejanos. It was situated on the waterfront and a lot of our teacher friends ate there on Friday night.

Lobster By The Ounce

One time we dined at the restaurant Harbor View. It was on the top of the island, maybe 800 feet above the ocean. They kept lobsters in a tank and encouraged patrons to pick out the ones they wanted. They were priced by the ounce so we were pleased to order the largest in the tank. OOPS!!! Price tag shock. When our friends Ted and Bess Adolphsen visited us, we took them to Harbor View for supper one night. You can see all of the harbor and the town and lights from up there. Beautiful view!!!

Roger, Lobster and the Royal Mail Inn

One time we went over the the Royal Mail Inn. It was located on an island in the middle of Charlotte Amalie Harbor. You take a ferry boat to it and back. We met our friend Roger there for dinner. Betty and I both ordered lobster and Roger looked over the menu for some time and ordered the same as we had. I don't think Roger, who was from the island, had ever seen lobster delivered to the table. He took one look at that Ug-Lee Ting and rose from the table and headed for the bar. Never saw him any more that night. (Never mentioned the matter to him.)

Lenny and Helene's Pool Party

Lenny, a counselor at the school and Helene, Betty's Reading Department Chairman, held a teacher's party at their home. We were encouraged to bring our swim suits as they had a fresh water pool. We all brought food for a pot luck dinner. We also brought plenty of alcoholic beverages. As the night wore on I got out my guitar and we had a minor "Hootenanny". We also spent a great deal of time in a ping pong tourney. After a while I noticed that I had visited the bar enough to feel the effects a little.

I decided I needed to take a quick dip in the pool just to clear my head a little. As related earlier, I learned to swim in the ocean. I knew the salinity of the ocean because of the taste. What I had never considered was the buoyancy of the salt water. In my bathing suit I closed my eyes and jumped into the pool on the deep end. I had worked up a sweat and God!!! That cool water felt so good! I just relaxed every muscle in my body and waited for my head to pop out of the water. About that time I felt the bottom of the pool touch my rear end. I opened my eyes and realized I was still under water. I started to move my arms and nothing much happened. I was running out of air. **"If I die here at the bottom of their swimming pool Saint Paul will never let me in!!!"** With a mighty effort I pushed off the bottom and my head cleared the surface, coughing and spitting and breathing I saved my own life. "Phew, that was a close one!" Then, looking around to make sure no one had seen my desperate situation I casually sauntered over and got another Heinekin. Shaking my head up and down, "Great Party"!!!

Mongoose for dinner

We made friends with a nice young couple from the Eastern seaboard. He was a P.E. teacher and she was a professional painter who specialized in painting little girls with large eyes. They invited us over to their apartment for steaks on the Barbeque. We were sitting on the patio, overlooking a valley of "BUSH", imbibing in a rum and coke or two, waiting for the coals to heat up. I commented on the beautiful steak they had sitting on the brick bench surrounding the living area. "Yeah, they had a special on these huge steaks down at Grand Union. I though I'd get one, cook it up and cut it up into four pieces." Just then a rather large mongoose climbed up and took the steak over the bench into the "Bush". What the heck...SALAD and more rum.

Dining Out In The "Bush"

We heard about a restaurant out in the "Bush" that was gaining quite a reputation. We decided to try out the place. Even though it is a small island, you can get lost in the bush. It took us some time to find the place. We got there and were guided to a table with two chairs. We sat down and he took our drink order. He suggested the specialty of the house which was made in a ceramic pineapple with a variety of tropical juices and rum and gin and something else extremely alcoholic. It came with two straws and an umbrella. "Expecting Rain? Whooo!!! That is strong. Just give us a minute or two to look over the menu." He left. I looked up at the fishnet covered ceiling and noticed a rat climbing around overhead. I knew I hadn't had that much of the drink. I signaled the waiter. "There's a rat right up there over our heads."

"Oh, that's that damn Henry. He's up there again."

He left. He returned. He had a shotgun. He aimed over our table. "Hey, wait a minute. What are you going to do?" The roar of the shotgun was deafening. His mouth was moving as though he was speaking. We couldn't hear anything. Dirt, pieces of rope, various parts of nautical equipment came raining onto our table. No rat. He missed. We left.

A Little Brush With Fame

One evening in our second floor condo we heard a loud speaker out on the beach or on the water in the bay. From our porch we could see the water in the harbor. Out in the water there were a lot of lights on a pretty good sized boat. At first we couldn't understand what they were saying but we could hear the voices carrying across the water as clear as a bell. Then we realized they were yelling in French. It was Jacques Cousteau's famous boat "The Calypso"!!! They had been diving further out and one of the men had a case of the "Bends". They had brought him to the harbor and the harbor medical crew had met them with a decompression chamber. The next morning we realized that the crew from "The Calypso" were staying in two apartments under us for a little while. They seemed to be quite nice folks but communication with them was a little stinted.

The End Game

We felt that the Virgin Island Department of Education was more than fair in dealing with Mainland teachers. Its policy was to pay for the teacher's transportation to the island and if the teacher was employed for two or not more than three years it would pay their way back home. By the time we signed on for the third year we knew it was time to go back home to Montana. Our friends, Ted and Bess Adolphsen had come to visit us. That had been a very enjoyable taste of "Back Home". Betty's mother, Mary, had popped in on us for a short visit. That had been nice. We had been over to Puerto Rico and back via the "Goose" (A water landing and take-off prop job). While there we had been priviledged to attend Sammy Davis Jr. in a casino performance of Mr. Bojangles. But other than our sailing we had not been off-island for going on three years. Seventeen miles long and three miles wide...you get to feeling a little landlocked.

The Bag End

We bought our little 25 foot sloop, The Bag End, for $2500. We had taken good care of her and she had faithfully taken us on many exploratory adventures and treated us with a lot of TLC. Now it was time to see her handed over to someone who would be her new caregiver. We posted a for sale sign on the teacher's board and one day later Terry, a counselor at school said he would be interested. He was happy to pay $2500 for her. We had sailed her for over two years and were excited to sell her for what we had paid for her. We took her out for one last sail. We noticed that the sea creatures were once again building up on her hull. We didn't get the full speed out of her. Well, Terry would have to scrape her...a good way to get acquainted.

We sailed for one last time back into the harbor, threading past the moored boats, past our hurricane anchorage buoy, brought her hard a-lee and with sails luffing drew up perfectly to our spot. Betty and Larry Jr. caught the buoy with the boat hook and fastened her down for the last time. We took our dingy over to the pier and got in our little "Bug" and wordlessly drove back home.

The Bug

We had to take care of the little VW that had carried us all over the island. Of course we had paid it off through the bank. The Education Department had taken payments out of our first of two checks we had received monthly and we were done paying after 18 months. I posted it for sale on the teachers bulletin board. No nibbles. If I sold it directly to a buyer, I could recapture the retail value. If I had to sell it to a dealer the best I could expect would be wholesale price. Well, down to the dealer across from the Chase Manhattan Bank I go. It has been 3 years...The same guy I "bought" it from couldn't possibly still be here. He would have gone back to New York City long ago. I drove into the used car lot like I owned it. You won't believe who came tripping out of the little shack. YES!!! The same guy!!! Oh Man!!!

"Hi. What can I do for you today?"

I surveyed his face, his eyes, his general posture. Everything seemed like a go!

"Well, We're leaving the island in about 10 days and we need to sell this beautiful little automobile." So far, so good. No sign of recognition.

"Say, don't I know you from somewhere?" asked the salesman, a slight frown furrowing his brow.

"Hmmm! Can't say we've met. I've been teaching out on the East end of the island for some time. You might have seen me playing in a carnival parade of something. Anyway, I have a special request to make of you in the purchase of this car. I'd like to simply drop it off with you on our way to the airport a week from Thursday, if you could give us a ride the rest of the way. What do you think?"

"Oh, now I remember you. You are the guy that almost cost me my job. I was brand new and you drove this very car right off the lot."

"I was kind of hoping you wouldn't be here any more."

With a light chuckle, he said, "Well, well, well. How much do you think its worth?"

All things considered, he was quite amiable and agreed to pay wholesale value and throw in the free ride to the airport. Man oh man, we were really getting ready to leave the islands for good.

Personal Effects

We got cardboard shipping boxes for the special twelve piece set of Dansk, earthenware dinnerware and Orrefer Chrystal Stemware and packaged it for shipping. The island was one of the few places on earth one could buy that kind of luxury merchandise with no duty attached. Likewise, we packaged our complete stereo set of Pioneer speakers, Tape player, Cassette player, Receiver and Garrard Turntable for shipment. We couldn't take a lot of the things we had purchased back on the plane, so we had to ship it home separately. A little expensive but worth it.

So, sure enough the day had come to leave the island. We bundled one suitcase each, two sets of golf clubs (unused in 3 years), one well used guitar and my old reliable portable typewriter into the car, said goodbye to our wonderful house, took one last look at the lonely little sloop down in the harbor, got in the car and left.

I estimate that we left the island perhaps a little touched by our hands, but we three knew the islands left an imprint on us that left our lives forever changed.

A couple of days later, our airplane was on final approach to the Billings Logan International Airport. As we banked left, we looked down and saw the Yellowstone River working its way East and South. All the emotions seemed to boil up in us. It had been three years since we had seen HOME.

Epilogue

I'm sitting here at my computer over 40 years later, trying to convey how I feel using words in the English language. All I know is that I have had the distinct privilege to teach in many schools and experience many people and their talents and personalities. Each place I have worked has shaped me and made me ready for whatever the next adventure was going to be. I don't believe any 3 year period in my life was filled with as much excitement, pleasure and sense of adventure as our time in the U.S.V.I.

We have never been back to this day. Now we are at a time of life that we may not ever get to return. It is my fondest wish that this little narrative will prompt someone to dare it. Bon Voyage!!!

www.ingramcontent.com/pod-product-compliance
Lightning Source LLC
Chambersburg PA
CBHW031432040426
42444CB00006B/778